*Guided by the
rhythm of nature*

ANNA LINDER

Guided by the rhythm of nature

FIRST EDITION, FULLCOLOUR HARDCOVER 2023

SECOND EDITION, PAPERBACK 2024

ISBN 9798335910064

THE CONTENTS OF THIS BOOK WERE FIRST PUBLISHED AS

EIGHT SEPARATE GUIDES STARTING IN 2020 AND HAVE SINCE

BEEN DISTRIBUTED FOR FREE THROUGHOUT EACH SEASON OF

THE WHEEL OF THE YEAR.

SET IN NOTO SANS AND PLAYFAIR DISPLAY

COVER PHOTO BY FREDRIK POSSE VIA UNSPLASH.

ANNA LINDER, AUTHOR & DESIGNER

MAGNITUD, KVARNVÄGEN 2J, 53030 TUN, SWEDEN

ANNALINDER.COM

"We can no longer hear the voice of

the rivers, the mountains, or the sea.

The trees and meadows are no longer

intimate modes of spirit presence.

The world about us has become an

'it' rather than a 'thou.'"

Thomas Berry - The Great Work

Acknowledgements

In the realm of gratitude, I find myself deeply thankful to two extraordinary individuals who have added enchantment and magick to my journey.

REBECCA ANUWEN *is a true teacher who revealed the beauty of the rhythms of the moon and the seasons to me. Her wisdom and guidance have enriched my life, and I'm eternally grateful.*

MOUNA BOUSLOUK, *a dear friend, is the catalyst for this book coming into being. Her unwavering encouragement and enthusiasm have been the driving light that transformed this project into a book.*

To both of you, I extend my heartfelt thanks for your enchanting presence in my life.

Content

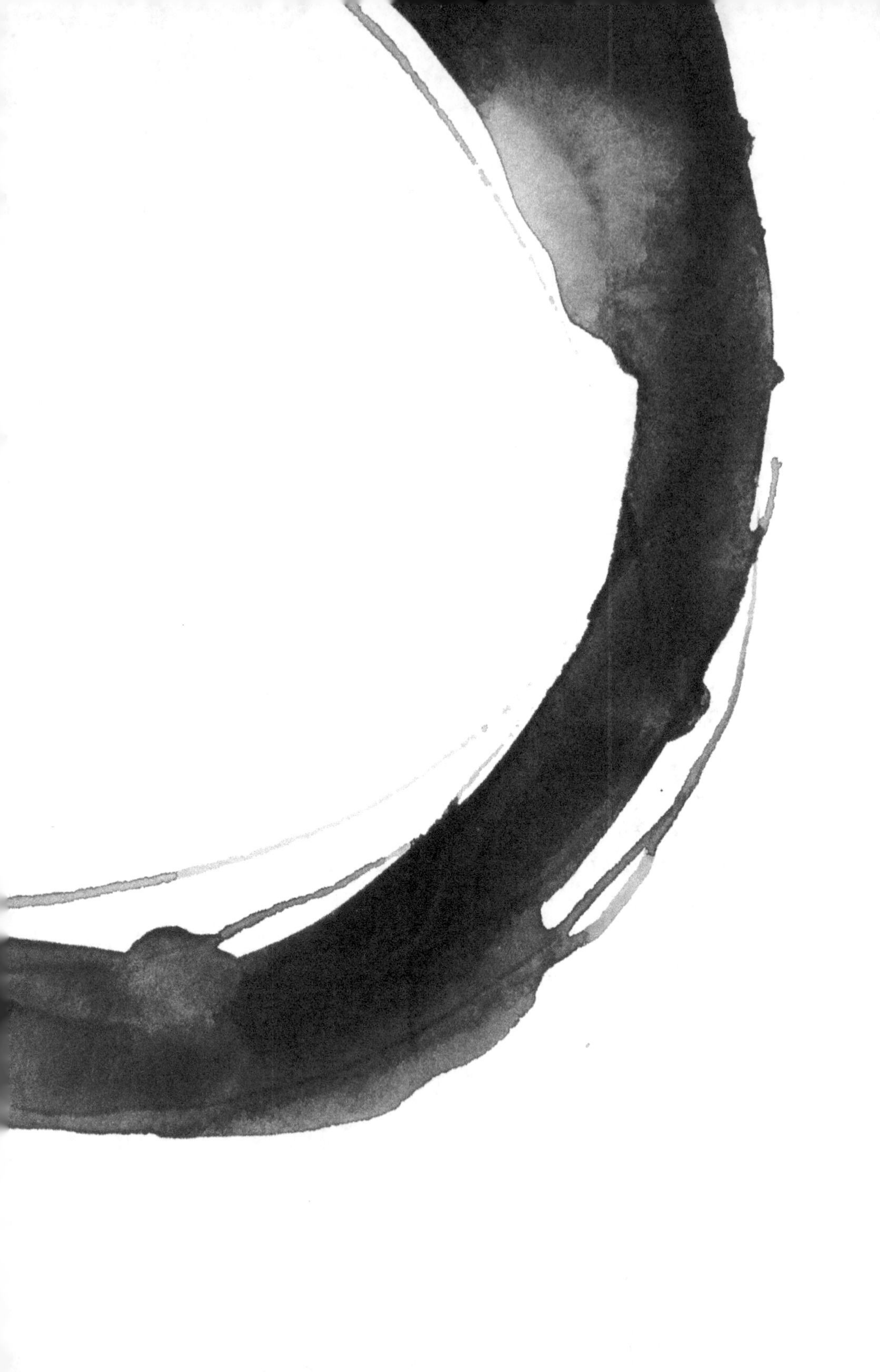

A seasonal rhythm

It was not until I lived in the middle of nature that my body reminded me that I needed balance– deep, deep recovering balance.

And with the shifting energy of the landscape surrounding me, it became impossible to live in a way that did not interact with the whispers of nature.

Over the years, I have, step by step, gained knowledge on how I am affected by the changes of the season, when my energy is high or low, when I feel powerful and strong, and when I need to take care of myself.

This guide is my attempt to get you curious about finding your unique rhythm.

– Anna Linder

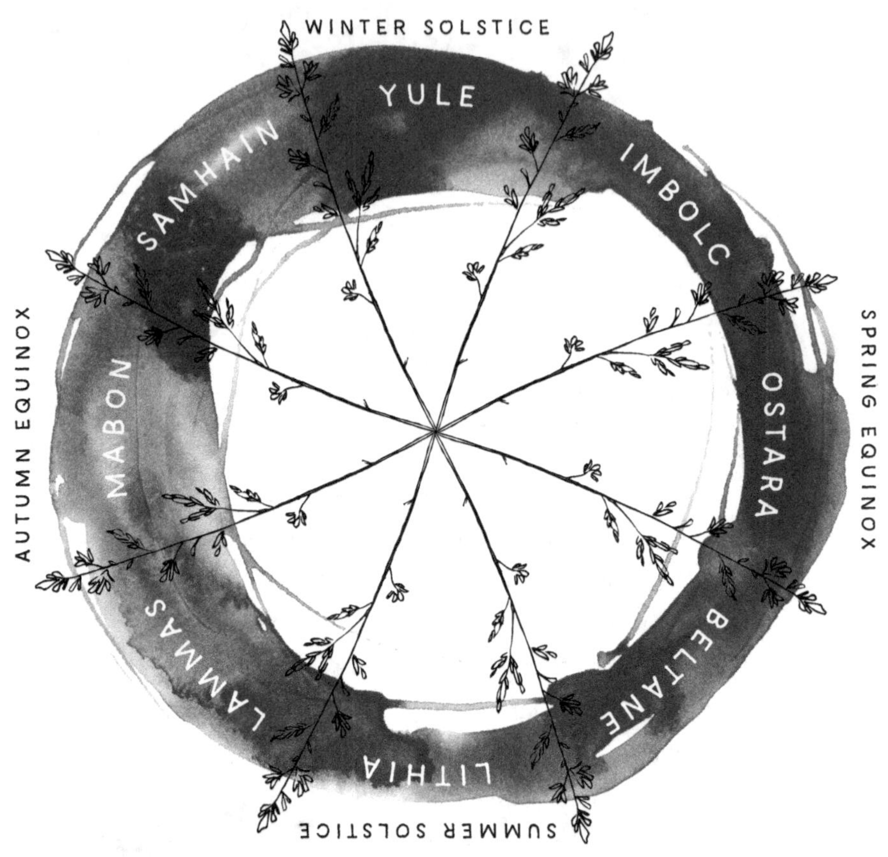

	NORTHERN HEMISPHERE	SOUTHERN HEMISPHERE
SAMHAIN	October 31–November 1	April 30–May 1
YULE | WINTER SOLSTICE	December 21/22	June 20/21
IMBOLC	February 2	August 1
OSTARA | SPRING EQUINOX	March 19/22	September 21/22
BELTANE	May 1	November 1
LITHA | SUMMER SOLSTICE	June 20/22	December 20/23
LAMMAS	August 1	February 1/2
MABON | AUTUMNAL EQUINOX	September 22/23	March 20/21

The Wheel of the year

The Wheel of the Year is a cyclical calendar based on pagan and nature-based beliefs and rituals. Its roots are unclear, but it's closely related to the old Celtic calendar, which revolves around eight festivals. The eight parts are based in Mother Earth's rhythms and the interplay between nature, the sun, and the moon.

As a seasonal guide, it helps us become more aware of changes in the environment and when attuning ourselves to the Wheel of the Year, we can become more mindful of our own rhythms and needs in harmony with the changing seasons.

Winter, spring, summer and fall - seasons we all know but do not always think of as guides that can create rhythm, energy and balance in life.

If we add four midpoints between the solstices and equinoxes, we get the Wheel of the Year.

Eight opportunities to pay attention to the changes of the seasons, the rhythm and shifts in nature, and a beginning to feel them within ourselves.

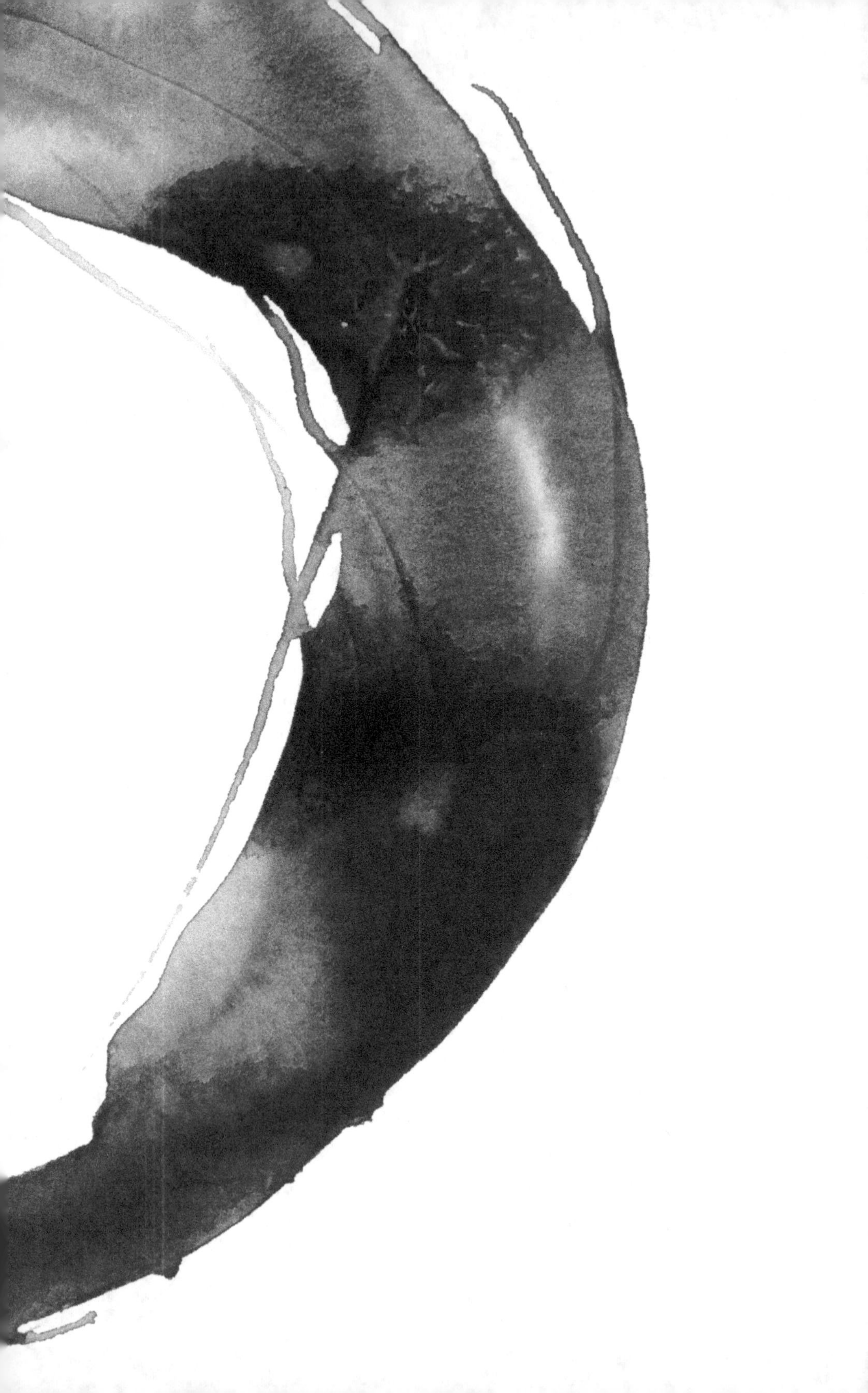

Samhain

EMBRACE THE DARKNESS & REST

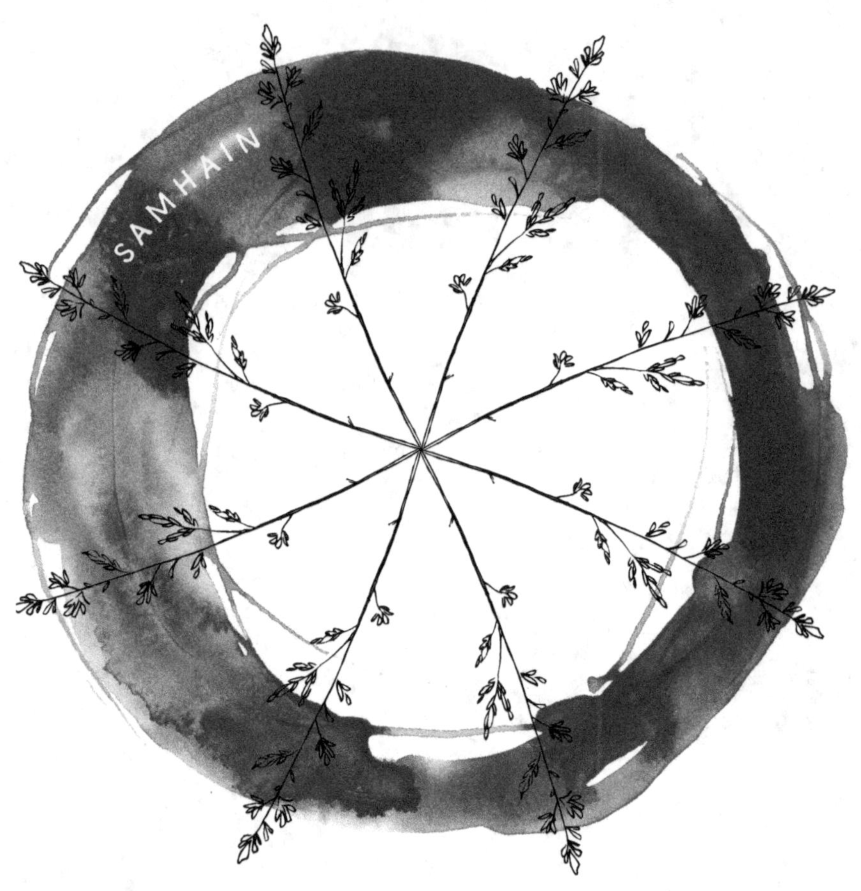

NORTHERN HEMISPHER

October 31 to December 20

SOUTHERN HEMISPHER

April 30 to June 19

Embrace the darkness & rest

The days are getting shorter, the darkness becomes deeper. Looking to nature, we notice that the trees have let their leaves fall and now provide the earth with a protective shield. Frost bites the vegetation, and the first snowfall is not far away.

We are in between the autumnal equinox and the winter solstice, the darkest phase of the year.

Nature rests, the roots gather strength, and, like nature, we humans need a period for rest, review, reflection, and closure. And magick.

Honour,
celebrate
&
embrace
darkness

This time of the year the veil between our world and the world of the dead is at its thinnest. It's a time to honour and celebrate our ancestors.

Samhain is also the beginning of the new year for witches and pagans. The harvest seasons end, we say goodbye to the sun and embrace the darkness.

HONOUR & CELEBRATE YOUR ANCESTORS

Add an extra seat when you set the table on October 31st and let one of your ancestors join you at the table.

Visit or invite one of your older living relatives and let them speak about their lives, memories and tell the story about your family.

EMBRACE THE DARKNESS

Spend time in nature at night. Or let the darkness surround you at home. And sit *with* the darkness.

What happens within you? With your thoughts? Do you want to run away, go deeper? What do you feel? How does your body react?

Rest

We are in between autumnal equinox and winter solstice, the darkest time of the year. Nature is resting, the animals prepare for hibernation - what do you do?

Do you push through at the same pace and do whatever it takes to stay on top of "everything"? How long is your to-do list, and how many "I'm just going to" do you need to complete before you're done? When will you get time to rest?

Sleeping through this time of the year is probably not an option (although the thought may be tempting), but how can you provide yourself with some rest?

Rest can be slowing down, creating space in your calendar, allowing yourself to do things at a slower pace, and being present in the moment with family or friends.

WHAT DO YOU NEED RIGHT NOW PHYSICALLY, MENTALLY, AND SPIRITUALLY?

IS REST AND RECOVERY SOMETHING THAT FEELS UNREACHABLE NOW? WHY?

Explore

What expression has nature, where you live, this time of the year?

You don't need to have access to deep forests, unbroken views or even a garden to explore the rhythm of nature. Just step outside and notice how the air feels against your skin, in your nostrils and how it affects you.

Add a tree, some shrubs or a small park that you see more or less on a daily basis and pay attention to the shifts and changes.

Add all the senses, the scent of the earth, the colours of the foliage and how the ground feels under your feet.

What signals do you get? How does the energy feel? And does it affect you?

I thrive in the darkness, with the grey overcast days and the high air on a clear morning. The calm of nature gives me a sense of inner peace, and I can relax in a way that I find difficult during any other season.

This is when I make time to reconnect with myself and my body and create a clear path for my mind.

THE CHANGING SEASONS AND SHIFTS IN NATURE AFFECT US ALL BUT IN DIFFERENT WAYS.

HOW DO YOU EXPERIENCE THIS TIME OF THE YEAR WHEN THE DAYS GET SHORTER

AND THE DARKNESS SURROUNDS US? HOW DO YOU ACT AND REACT?

DEFY THE WEATHER.

Go out as much as you can. Nothing clears the mind like a walk where the weather is the most prominent factor. And enjoy the pleasure to get back into the warmth.

LIGHT, LIGHT AND MORE LIGHT.

We know this, but it's easy to forget the simple things. Let in the daylight and light candles and even more candles when darkness falls.

WANDER

When the sky is clear and the air high, wander. Walking without a goal or a purpose can be the most difficult or the easiest thing there is. Look up, look down, stroll onto a new path or stop and close your eyes to experience the scents.

Review
Reflect
Release

Samhain is a period of death and rebirth, closure and release, and rest. A time to look back at the year that has passed from different perspectives and leave behind what no longer serves us.

There is no one right way to do this and if you have your own process, stay with it.

If not, the following pages invite you to explore, ponder and discern. Putting words to what is going on in your head is one way to explore – expressing yourself with colours and shapes is another. Some questions might need to be processed in your mind for a while.

Create your way.

Do it at your pace.

And only if you want to.

WHAT ARE YOUR STRONGEST MEMORIES OF THIS YEAR?

HOW DID THAT AFFECT YOU?

WHO HAS BEEN IMPORTANT TO YOU DURING THE YEAR?

WHAT DID THEY MAKE YOU FEEL / DO AND HOW DID THAT SUPPORT YOU?

WHAT DO YOU THINK YOU HAVE LEARNED ABOUT YOURSELF?

I HAVE EXPLORED

I HAVE EMBRACED

I HAVE LEFT BEHIND

I HAVE LEARNT TO SAY NO TO

I HAVE LEFT BEHIND

Release

Release

Magick

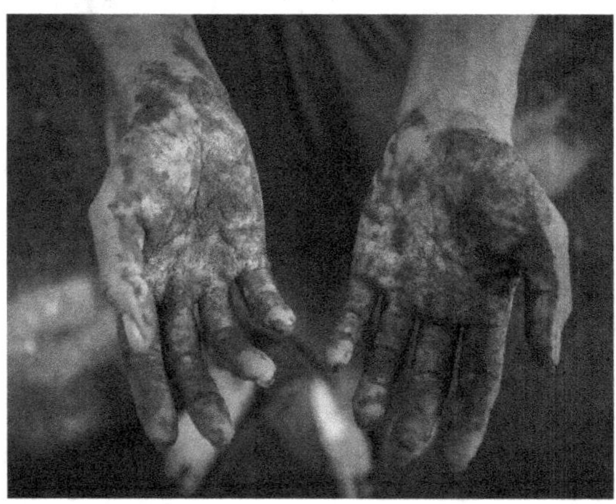

To mark an ending it's a good idea to physically get rid of what you no longer want to carry with you.

On a piece of paper, write, draw or create something that represents what you want to let go of or leave behind.

Burning (in a safe way) the words, the drawing or the creation is one way to mark a symbolic ending, but there are more ways.

Listen to your intuition and instinct, and you will know what you need to do.

BEGINNING

Let tarot or oracle cards guide you on the upcoming year. Draw eight cards – one for each season and sabbat in the Wheel of the Year.

THE SPIRAL

Gather material from nature and create a spiral. Imagine yourself at the centre, moving outwards, towards the light, and returning back into the darkness at the centre of the spiral. Do you feel drawn or more at home at a specific stage in the spiral?

Midwinter
TEND TO THE ROOTS TO FIND THE SEEDS

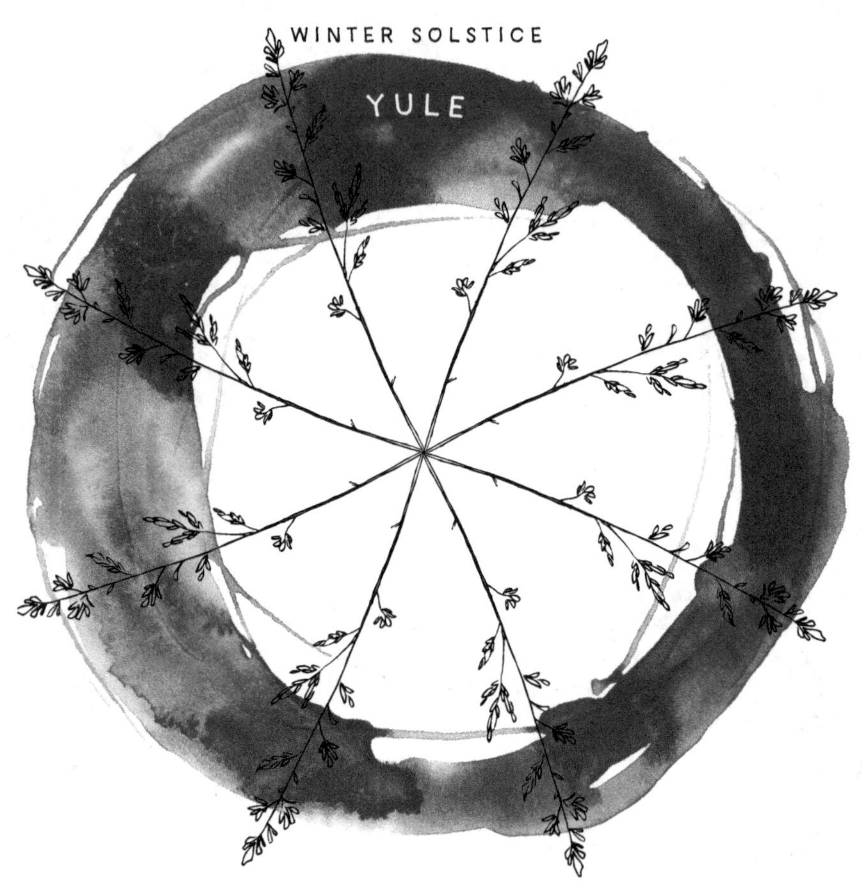

NORTHERN HEMISPHERE

December 21st to Feburary 1st

SOUTHERN HEMISPHERE

June 20/21 to July 31st

Nourishment from within

If we turn our attention to nature at this time of the year, it may seem like nothing is going on - but beneath the surface, nature is preparing for Spring to come.

Deep into the earth seeds rest, seeds that need to be nourished in order to come to life and bloom. Leaves, fallen branches, dried plants and soil provides a protective layer for hibernating animals and insects.

As humans, we also need to tend to what is deep within us before we create promises, goals and plans for the turns of the wheel of the year.

Just like nature, this is a period to provide ourselves with nourishment, care and strength — from within — before we start on new ideas, activities and projects.

The longest night

The darkest day or the longest night — it might be a day you barely endure or it will be a day when you give yourself a pause, light candles and take a moment to go inward.

A STANDSTILL

When you almost have lost faith that the light ever will return, the sun reaches its lowest point and for a couple of days seems to stand still - to begin climbing again as the days grow longer.

Make time for yourself, if only for a moment, to find your way back home into yourself and your body. Pay attention to what you need. Do you crave silence, peace and time alone? Or time spent with those closest to you, two or four-legged.

If the night brings you a clear sky, wander out and look at the starry sky. The Midwinter night is said to be filled with magic - what wishes do you want to send to the universe?

HONOUR THE LIGHT

The winter solstice marks the darkest day and the longest night of the year. At the same time, it is the point when the wheel of the year turns and light and life returns.

Lighting candles in all windows, creating an altar with gold and white candles is a simple way to honour and welcome Mother Sun.

Nourishment

Winter solstice, the darkest day of the year, starts this period, and in the northern hemisphere, it's the end of December, a period marked by family traditions and filled with expectations. For many, it can be a time when we are drained of energy.

Trying to balance everything that pulls us in different directions and at the same time attempt to start new ways around well-being, relationships, career and spare time can feel overwhelming.

Nourishing ourselves can begin with the tiniest steps to awaken curiosity and an inner flame that makes us want to take care of ourselves.

Allow energy and strength to be created from within, as the roots of the trees and the core of the seed, growing from what is really truly important to us.

 I have a tendency to spread myself thin and then some, and land in a place of not being able to do anything. So often I need to scale away and scale down, and time and time again, go back to the basics - eight hours of sleep, food that is good for me and some form of movement. I easily forget to have a holistic approach to my health and well-being and turn to quick fixes.

HOW DO YOU TAKE CARE OF YOURSELF PHYSICALLY, MENTALLY, EMOTIONALLY AND
SPIRITUALLY?

DO YOU FEEL A RESISTANCE TO GIVE YOURSELF CARE AND LOVE? WHY?

Explore

How does nature express itself where you live, this time of the year?

You don't need to have access to deep forests, unbroken views or even a garden to explore the rhythm of nature. Just step outside and notice how the air feels against your skin, in your nostrils and how it affects you.

If you have the possibility, find a tree, some shrubs or a small park that you see more or less on a daily basis and pay attention to the shifts and changes.

Add all the senses, the scent of the earth, the colours of the foliage and how the ground feels under your feet.

What signals do you get? How does the energy feel? And does it affect you?

REFLECTION *I dream about the snow-filled winters of my childhood when my whole world turned into a special kind of magic and beauty. Now I try to find magic by befriending the trees around me. Observing the birch catkins wait for warmth. Noticing how the evergreen firs and pines and the proud oak provide the squirrels with winter food.*

THE CHANGING SEASONS AND SHIFTS IN NATURE AFFECT US ALL BUT IN DIFFERENT WAYS. HOW DO YOU EXPERIENCE THIS TIME WHEN THE LIGHT SLOWLY RETURNS AND A NEW YEAR BEGINS? HOW DO YOU ACT AND REACT?

Settle down in a comfortable position somewhere you can be undisturbed. Take a few breaths. Notice where there is tension in your body.

Turn your attention to your feet, create tension in all muscles in your feet and toes - hold this for a few seconds and then release the tension.

Continue with the calf muscle, the whole lower leg, thigh muscle, buttocks, abdomen, chest, shoulders, arms, hands, neck and face.

Tighten, keep the tension and relax.

Sometimes it can feel impossible to release the tension, reinforce by saying words like release, open, relax

Take a deep breath and observe if your body feels different than when you began.

Stay. Try to be in touch with your body. If you have a hot drink you can wrap your hands around it. Let your eyes wander across the room, out the window. Breathe in. Breathe out.

Caringly
Curiously
Closely

Midwinter is a time to turn inward and provide vitality to new life. As in nature, the seeds within you needs to be nourished in order to be able to come to life and bloom.

This is a period when we can create a foundation of fertile soil and become curious about our own life. And provide ourselves with nourishment, strength and care – from within – before we take the step and show the world what we want, wish and intend to do.

There is no one right way to do this and if you have your own process, stick with it.

If not, the following pages invite you to explore, ponder and discern.

Create your way.

Do it at your pace.

And only if you want to.

MY BODY LONGS FOR

MY HEART AND SOUL WANTS

I AM AFRAID OF

THIS MAKES ME SMILE

THIS FILLS ME WITH ENERGY

THIS MAKES ME SAD OR DRAINS ME OF ENERGY

HOW DO YOU WANT TO SPEND YOUR TIME? WHY?

WHAT DO YOU WANT MORE SPACE FOR? WHY?

Curious

IF YOU TURN BACK TO YOUR ANSWERS ON THE PREVIOUS PAGES - CAN YOU FIND
SOMETHING THERE THAT CAN BE A SEED TO DEVELOP? SOMETHING YOU WOULD LIKE
TO SEE BECOME A REALITY?

DO YOU HAVE OR CAN YOU CREATE PHYSICAL, MENTAL AND EMOTIONAL SPACE TO
REALISE IT?

Closely

Magick

DREAM & FIND THE SEEDS

This is a good time to start dreaming about and find the seeds for this year's garden of your life.

If you are in the northern hemisphere, let Christmas and New Year pass and the calm of January arrive.

- Take a walk and see which trees or plants capture your interest. Take a closer look and see what traces of coming life you can discover in and around them.
- Take care of your indoor plants, what do they need and does that remind you of something you need.
- Let the starry night sky inspire you to dream beyond what you think is possible.
- Make a tea full of flavour and aroma to stimulate your senses. Ginger, honey, cloves, cinnamon, orange peel and star anise create both fragrance and well-being this time of the year.

TINY SUNS AND WINTER LIGHTS

To welcome the sun and invite the light can be done in different ways and on several occasions during this period.

It doesn't only serve as a reminder of daylight, but also reminds us of our ability to light the flame and the fire within ourselves.

If you are lucky enough to live where there is snow, let the child in you make snow lanterns that light up the winter night or let citrus fruits become tiny indoor suns.

Imbolc
TO HURRY SLOWLY

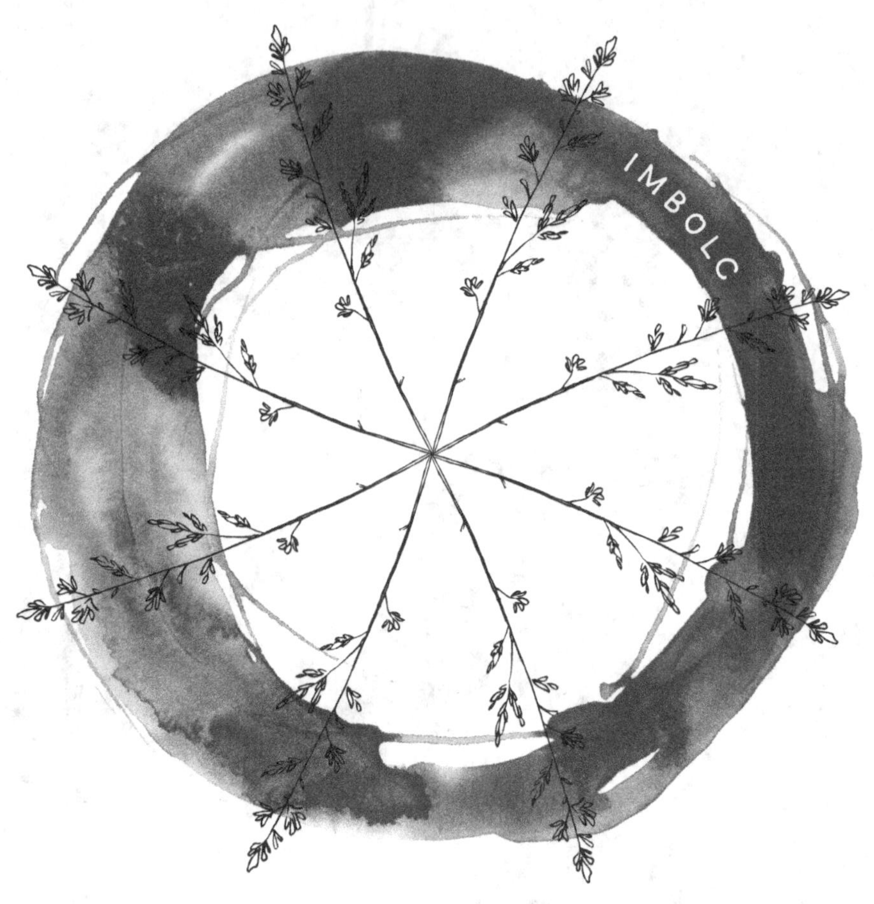

NORTHERN HEMISPHERE

February 2 to March 18/19

SOUTHERN HEMISPHERE

August 1 to September 21/22

To hurry slowly

We are at the midpoint between winter and spring, a fickle weather period when most of natures growth evolves underground, waiting for warmth and light.

Depending on where you live, spring can feel both very far away and just around the corner. Some of us will feel the first warming sunbeams standing against someone elses abundant snowfall.

For us humans, this time can create conflicting emotions, the energy begins to rise at the same time as we feel tired to the bone, impatiently we want to get going and simultaneously wanting to let things stay just as they are.

If we let nature guide us, we can embrace a way of hurry slowly and create space for what grows a little deeper within us.

Welcome
warmth
and light

Imbolc is the Celtic name for Cross-Quarter Day between the Winter Solstice and Spring Equinox. It is characterised by the literal meaning of the word - in the belly.

In the ground, the seeds start to turn so they can germinate, and within us, ideas and plans grow. During the Imbolc celebration, we show our longing for spring and welcome the return of warmth and light.

FIRE & WATER

Lighting a fire can be both a symbolic and practical event. After the winter rest, we may need to stoke our inner fire, chase away the darkness and stagnant energy. Gathering around an open outdoor fire and celebrate that light has won over darkness is one option. Turning on all the lamps and lighting candles at home is another.

Water in motion is a clear sign that spring is on its way and also a symbol of purification. Go out in nature and find a stream, river or open water - dip all, or part of yourself, and take note of how it affects your energy.

IDUN & BRIGID

In Nordic tradition, Idun is the bearer of light and spring; in Celtic it is Brigid. Both represent fertility, hope and creativity. Celebrate them by making your own symbols of creativity and fertility.

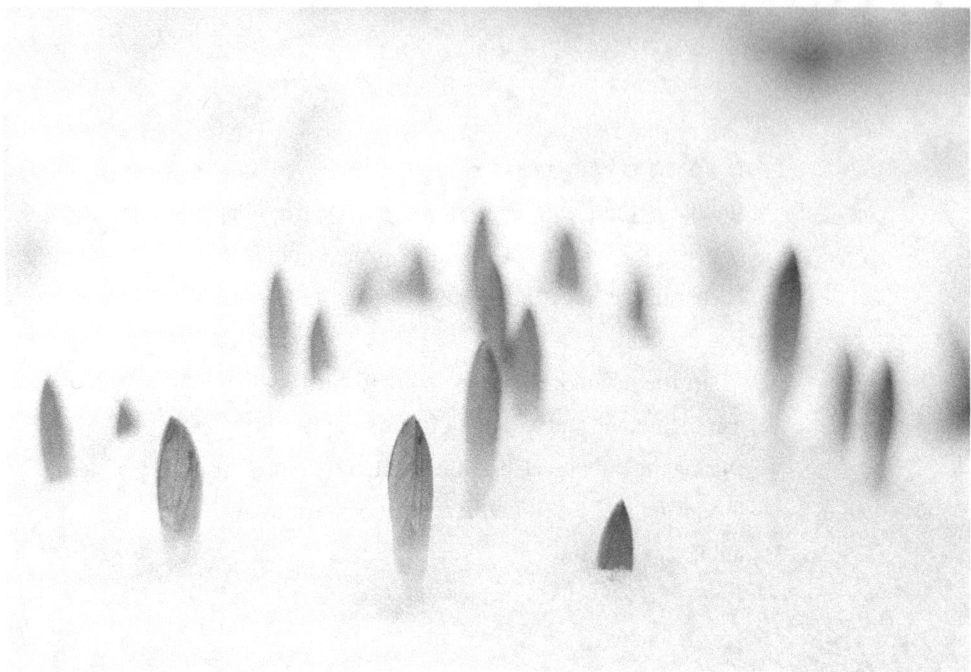

Create space

In times of transition and change, such as the period between winter and spring, we may feel pressured to get started on everything at once and go from zero to a hundred with endless to-do lists. Maybe both because we want to and because we feel we should.

If we look to nature, we see that everything doesn't unfurl or begin to bloom at the same time. We are also aware that nothing grows strong if it does not get off to a good start. Creating space for new things to emerge is both about clearing out the old and nourishing the new.

And maybe even prune a bit among all the new ideas, projects and musts.

WHAT'S IN MOST NEED OF NOURISHMENT FOR YOU RIGHT NOW - THE PHYSICAL, MENTAL, EMOTIONAL OR SPIRITUAL?

DOES ANY PART OF YOUR LIFE OR YOU NEED MORE TIME TO REST?

Explore

How does nature appear where you are right now? What is happening in the nature around you at this time of year? What can you see with the naked eye, and what can you sense?

You don't need to have access to deep forests, unbroken views or even a garden to explore the rhythm of nature. Just step outside and notice how the air feels against your skin, in your nostrils and how it affects you.

Paying attention to the changes in one specific place over time is another way to begin to approach the rhythm of nature.

Add all the senses, the scent of the earth, the colours and how the ground feels beneath your feet.

What signals do you get? How does the energy feel? And does it affect you?

It fascinates me how plants have the power to emerge through the snow and let their buds be nourished by the light that is available this time of year. The longing for light is strong, and we northerners are known for defying the cold to enjoy the first warming rays of the sun. The first cup of coffee outdoors – pure bliss!

THE CHANGING SEASONS AND SHIFTS IN NATURE AFFECT US ALL BUT IN DIFFERENT WAYS. HOW DO YOU EXPERIENCE THIS TIME BETWEEN WINTER AND SPRING, A BEGINNING AND AN END AND NEW ENERGY? HOW DO YOU ACT AND REACT?

This time of the year, media is filled with guides on what we should do to detox, become energy-filled and happy. Just the thought of getting started can be overwhelming. So make it simple and do the small things.

- Dance - two minutes of crazy dancing can uplift the mood.
- Turn on your favourite song and sing at the top of your lungs.
- Spice up your food - it increases circulation.
- Drink water - yes the constant advice, but it makes a difference.
- Add colour - spring flowers adds both colour and fragrance.
- Inhale. Exhale.

To breathe even more life into ourselves and our homes, open all windows and let new air refresh our rooms and lungs.

Insights
Space
Vitality

Flighty and hesitant and at the same time resolute and stable - nature knows where it is heading but this wintery springtime may feel a little ambivalent to us.

The yearning to see our seeds, literal or figurative, germinate and sprout is huge, and to hurry slowly is perhaps the last thing we want. If we let this period be filled by slowly creating insight, space and vitality for our dreams and ideas, I am convinced that it will give us an energy as strong as Spring itself.

There is no one right way to do this and if you have your own process, stick with it.

If not, the following pages invite you to explore, ponder and discern.

Create your way.

Do it at your pace.

And only if you want to.

DO YOU LIKE TO BEGINNINGS OR ENDINGS?

DOES IT FEEL EASY OR DIFFICULT FOR YOU TO ASK FOR HELP?

MUST & SHOULD OR NEED & WANT?

Insights

WHAT MUNDANE TASKS DO YOU TEND TO PUT TO THE SIDELINES?

WHAT EVERYDAY ROUTINES DO YOU WANT MORE ORGANIZED? HOW LONG WOULD IT TAKE TO GET THERE?

WHICH EVERYDAY TASKS TAKE UP MORE THINKING TIME THAN THEY ACTUALLY TAKE TO COMPLETE?

Space

WHAT DO YOU NEED TO BE ABLE TO GO FROM IDEA & PLANNING TO PRACTICAL ACTION?

WHAT DO YOU NEED TO BE ABLE TO CONCENTRATE AND BE PRESENT?

WHAT DO YOU NEED TOBE ABLE TO CREATE EMOTIONAL POWER AND WILLPOWER?

WHAT DO YOU NEED TO BE ABLE HEAR YOUR INNER VOICE AND TRUST YOUR INTUI-TION?

Vitality

Magick

When we shift from one season to another, we can feel out of alignment with the energy around us. To balance your energies may sound complex, a simple way is to use the four elements that are naturally present in, and around us.

Where or what do you feel stuck in? Which element do you instinctively feel has taken over or needs replenishment?

EARTH | THE SOLID ELEMENT

Stability, grounded, firm, security

Moves slow and steady.

When you need patience and gradual development.

Being; practical, reliable, determined, tenacious, sensual, hard-working

Connected to our physical body, the ground beneth us and the fertile soil.

AIR | THE ELUSIVE ELEMENTET

Light, adaptable, flexible, instable

Moves quickly.

When you need movement, rapid change, mental activity, ideas, interaction

Being; friendly, curious, adaptable, idealistic, talkative, imaginative.

Connected to our mind, the wind and our breath.

FIRE | THE ACTION ELEMENT

Activity, change, enthusiasm, vitality.

Moves rapidly.

When you need creativity, action, to make things happen.

Being; self-confident, passionate, impulsive, outgoing, vigorous, courageous.

Connected to our life force, fire, a burning flame and the power within.

WATER | THE MOVEMENT ELEMENTET

Purifying, healing, nurture, intuition.

Moves changeable.

When you need change, stimulation, movement, womb connection.

Being: emotional, sensitive, intuitive, imaginative, compassionate.

Connected to our emotions and all sources of water – open and contained.

Ostara
A BUDDING SENSATION

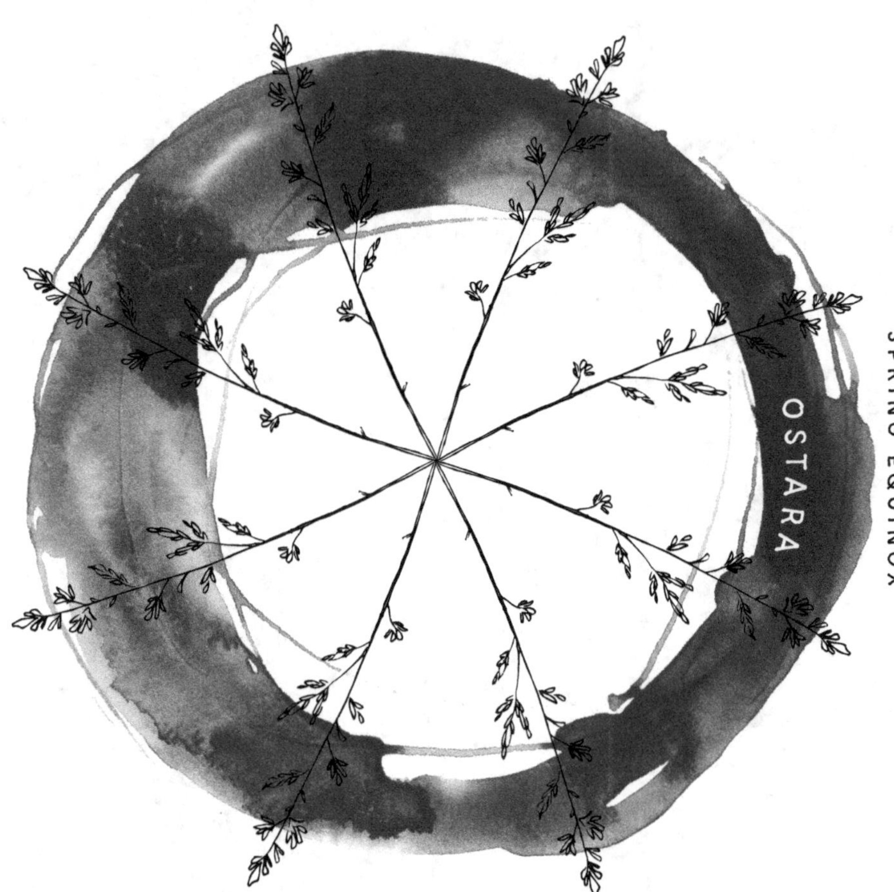

NORTHERN HEMISPHERE

March 20 to April 30

SOUTHERN HEMISPHERE

September 23 to October 31

A budding sensation

Spring feelings, the flickering hope that something new is coming, a fleeting longing, a budding sensation of endless possibilities yet unknown.

Being able to cherish that feeling and, just like nature, allow the roots to grow stable, the seeds to find the way into the light, and the buds to unfurl — can support a gentle start into the rising energy of the months ahead.

Spring is on its way, or maybe it has arrived, and we need energy to dream and sow the seeds of our yearnings, but also make sure that we have the stamina we need for them to bloom, bear fruit and be harvested.

Light
conque
the
dark

The spring equinox is one of the two points in the year wheel when day and night are equal, light and dark in balance. It is also the day when we know that the light will conquer over the darkness, the days will become longer and winter will turn into spring.

Ostara or Ēostre is said to be one of the fertility goddesses and if something is clearly reflected in the time during and after the spring equinox, it is the fertility and fruitfulness of the earth, the animals and nature.

GET OUT & GREET THE DAWN

Pack a simple breakfast and head out to meet the dawn this morning when night and day are equal.

When the sun rises above the horizon, think about what you want to hold onto from the darker months, and what you want to grow in the light.

FERTILITY AND NEW LIFE

Eggs are a symbol of both fertility and magic, during Ostara they can become the bearers of our intentions. Decorate them with symbols, words or colours that express what you want to grow, make bloom and harvest during the year.

Depending on your intention, eat them, bury them or use them as decorations.

Equilibrium

Springtime often becomes a period of taking action, a time focused on the explosive energy and doing — but early Spring is a time to foster equilibrium.

It's a time to create perseverance without draining ourselves. We need to let the energy flow but also know how to recuperate.

When we let nature be our guide, we will see that it awakens step by small step and that all plants do so at their own pace.

With this growing energy, attempt to create a fertile foundation and long-term sustainability so you have the strength to grow, sprout, bud and someday flower.

WHAT AREAS OF YOUR LIFE FEELS WELL-BALANCED? WHAT AREAS NEEDS ADJUSTING?

HOW CAN YOU NOURISH YOURSELF & TEND TO YOUR RECUPERATION?

SMALL CLUES:

DO YOU NEED SIMPLE PRACTICAL ROUTINES TO BRING EASE TO YOUR EVERYDAY LIFE?

DOES YOUR PHYSICAL BODY LONG FOR SOMETHING?

DO YOU FEEL DRAWN TO THE FOREST AND NATURE?

IS EMPTY TIME, QUIET MOMENTS AND GOING INWARD WHAT YOU NEED?

Explore

What does nature look like where you are? What is happening in the nature around you at this time of year? What trees leaf out the earliest? What flowers are visible? And how does the sun feel against your skin?

You don't need to have access to deep forests, unbroken views or even a garden to explore the rhythm of nature. Just step outside and notice how the air feels and how it affects you.

Paying attention to the changes, in one specific place, over time is another way to begin to approach the rhythm of nature.

Add all senses, the scent of the earth, the colours and how the ground feels beneath your feet.

What signals do you get? How does the energy feel? And does it affect you?

Spring feels like a time of expectations and I can become overwhelmed by everything that must, should and ought to happen. Remembering to continuously check in with myself becomes necessary. Is this important to me? Are these expectations mine or are they anticipations from the outside world? Letting go of the thoughts that everything needs be groundbreaking and massive helps me keep my feet on the ground.

THE CHANGING SEASONS AND SHIFTS IN NATURE AFFECT US ALL BUT IN DIFFERENT WAYS. HOW DO YOU EXPERIENCE THIS TIME WHEN ENERGY AND LIGHT INCREASE? HOW DO YOU ACT AND REACT?

SPRING CLEANING

The sun rays of spring can reveal dust and cobwebs — both in our homes and in our lives.

Is there an area in your life that you feel need a cleanse? Relationships that need a refresh? Or do you long for a shift of mindsets?

Make a quick inventory and see where you want to let new light in.

SMALL CHANGES

If we start to examine our routines and habits, we notice that simple changes to our everyday life can create new energy. We often, almost automatically, say no or yes and miss experiences and challenges that can become small everyday adventures.

Start small, take a new route home, try a new recipe and see how it feels.

Inspiration
Intention
Invitation

Spring is a time for dreaming, planting and experimentation. It's a time to be fueled by inspiration, set an intention, open up and invite momentum.

It is also a time to keep dreams alive with tender care and revise, reframe and allow trials and errors.

When we plant a seed in the dark soil we have to add something to make it grow. To create fertility we need to work with polar opposite forces. Yin & yang, dark & light, past & future, intention with action, fire and water, instinct and wisdom.

The same applies to making shifts and changes a reality in our own lives. We have to create room for, and be prepared to, work with opposing forces and the unknown.

There is no one right way to do this and if you have your own process, stick with it.

If not, the following pages invite you to explore, ponder and discern.

Create your way.

Do it at your pace.

And only if you want to.

DAYDREAM — WHAT HAPPENS WHEN YOU LET YOUR THOUGHTS FOLLOW THE WHISPERS OF YOUR HEART AND SOUL?

DOES DAYDREAMING FEEL LIKE A WASTE OF TIME? WHY?

Inspiration

WHEN DO YOU FEEL MOST LIKE YOURSELF?

WHAT IS INSPIRATIONAL TO YOU?

Inspiration

Intention

CAN YOU THINK OF SOMETHING THAT SEEMED IMPOSSIBLE BUT BECAME POSSIBLE?

DO YOU TREAT PROMISES TO YOURSELF AS SERIOUSLY AS PROMISES TO OTHERS?
WHY?

Intention

WHAT DO YOU TEND TO IGNORE OR AVOID?

WHEN DO YOU TEND TO STAY IN YOUR INTERNAL WORLD WHEN YOU NEED TO MOVE AND ACT?

IS THERE EVER A TIME WHEN GIVING UP MAKES SENSE?

Invitation

Magick

Magic and rituals on abundance, balance, change, clarity, fertility, growth, lust, beginnings and purification are in focus during this period.

Whatever you choose to do, make it special to you! The beautiful thing about magic is its ability to be and make it personal. When we take a moment and listen to ourselves we know what to do.

THE HARE

Look for the hare it's a major symbol of fertility and abundance. Why? She can conceive while pregnant.

And do not about forget the eggs — you can read about them on page 5.

PLANT AN INTENTIONAL SEED

Plant an actual seed together with an intention.

Choose something easy to grow, like sunflower, marigold, basil or cress.

Hold the seeds in your hands and set the intention. It can be something that you want to transform, grow or dream about — try to be specific.

Make sure to provide what they need, and see the intention and seed grow day by day.

Beltane
EVOKE PLEASURE

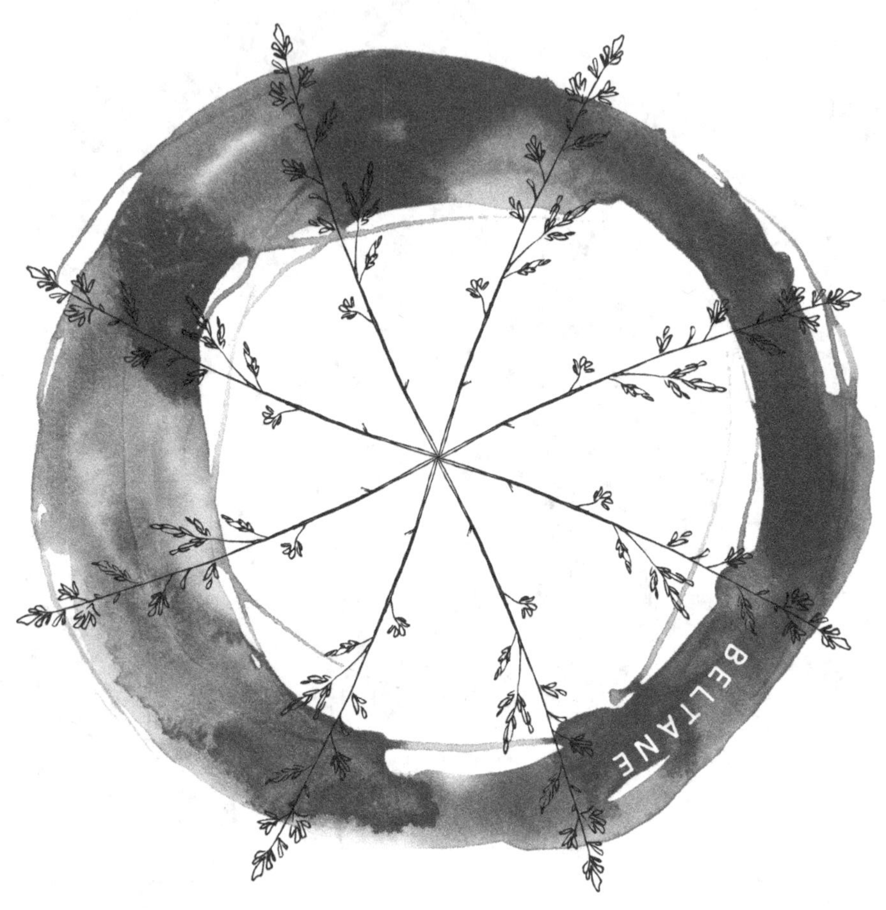

NORTHERN HEMISPHERE

May 1st to June 19/22

SOUTHERN HEMISPHERE

November 1st to December 19/22

Evoke pleasure

At the cross point between the rising energy from the Spring equinox on the way to its peak at Summer Solstice, Beltane arrives, and the nature around us explodes with life. It's far from hard to understand that this is a season filled with almost electric energy.

We can perceive it as if we constantly are on the verge of something and that we balance between being the container for an immense energy and letting it flow freely.

The experience can be positive or negative, it can create a wonderful momentum or make us lose our footing completely.

To enjoy this often tumultuous time, everything that grounds us, establishes contact with Mother Earth, figuratively or literally, can be helpful.

The fire of desire

At the cross point between Spring equinox and Midsummer, Beltane is the festival when life is honored, celebrated and maybe even created. It is a joyful, festive time in celebration of passion and pleasure.

THE FIRE OF DESIRE

There are four fire festivals during the year and Beltane is one of them.

Fire, a symbol of re-brith, bringing life to our own inner strengths, fertility and passion, and that is exactly what Beltane is about.

Let the bonfire become a symbol for what *you* want to bring to life and for the creative power you have within you, or let it clear the way so new energy can gain momentum and grow.

LIFE FORCE

This is a time when nature is bursting with life, and that gives us a chance to tap into that expansive energy.

Get outside, enjoy the sounds and scents of the forest, stay outside until the stars come to life or take a barefoot walk. Take your activities outdoor or just pause in the fresh air.

Pleasure

We all know how it feels to go, go, go, to look straight ahead and not "get side-tracked".

Imagine if you instead of pushing yourself to get going explored, engaged and enjoyed everything that gives you pleasure.

Take a different path for a moment, get a little lost and embrace the wild, raw, unknown, almost chaotic feeling that the energy during late spring and early summer has - if we stop and let it embrace us.

Do you dare to experiment, be a bit wilder and let the energy start flowing?

WHAT DO YOU NEED MOST OF ALL RIGHT NOW?

WHAT IS YOUR GUT REACTION TO THE WORDS PLEASURE AND LUST?

Explore

What does nature look like where you are? What is going on in your surroundings at this time of the year? Wich birds are chirping? What scents fill the air? And how does the wind feel against your skin?

You don't need to have access to deep forests, unbroken views or even a garden to explore the rhythm of nature. Just step outside and notice how the air feels and how it affects you.

Paying attention to the changes is another way to begin to approach the rhythm of nature.

If possible, find a tree, some shrubs or a small park that you see more or less on a daily basis and notice to the shifts and changes.

Add all senses, the scent of the earth, the colors and how the ground feels beneath your feet.

What signals do you get? How does the energy feel? And does it affect you?

THE CHANGING SEASONS AND SHIFTS IN NATURE AFFECT US ALL BUT IN DIFFERENT WAYS. HOW DO YOU EXPERIENCE THIS TIME WHEN WE BALANCE BETWEEN SPRING & SUMMER AND THE ENERGY IS HIGH? HOW DO YOU ACT AND REACT?

GROUNDING

Being grounded is to feel fully present in your body and/or feeling connected to the earth beneath you.

PUT YOUR HANDS IN WATER

Focus on the temperature of the water, how does it feel on your fingertips, palms, the backs of your hands. Does the sensation stay the same or does it shift on different parts of your hand?

TOUCH TREES, GRASS, FLOWERS

Are the things you touch soft or hard? Heavy or light? Warm or cool? Notice textures and structures and how they feel.

LISTEN TO YOUR SURROUNDINGS

Take a moment to really listen to the sounds and noises around you. What do you hear? Traffic? Birds? Dogs barking? Wind? Listen in again, can you hear beneath the most obvious sounds?

BAREFOOT

Take a slow walk barefoot and make yourself aware of the sensations in your toes and feet.

HEAD AND FEET

Place one hand on the top of your head and let your awareness sink into your feet.

Express
Experiment
Embrace

Nature doesn't make it self small - it takes up space, it blooms and sways and grows and give. It set roots, seeks light and create shadows.

What would happen if we lived our lives with more pleasure and enjoyment and dared to explore that more? How would life feel if you made time to be a bit wild? What would happen if you turned an average Wednesday into a small adventure?

Or what if you started to express and embrace what you feel deep inside?

No need to start a revolution (unless you want to), or change your life completely, this energetic season is a great time to express what you long for, experiment, break a habit and maybe find something new within yourself.

There is not one right way to do this and if you have your own process, stick with it.

If not, the following pages invites you to explore, ponder and discern.

Create your way.

Do it at your pace.

And only if you want to.

WHEN DO YOU FEEL SAFE EXPRESSING YOUR DESIRES AND LONGINGS?

WHEN DO YOU FEEL MOST VULNERABLE? WHY?

DO YOU FIND IT EASY OR DIFFICULT TO EXPRESS YOUR VIEWS, IDEAS AND THOUGHTS?

WHAT DESIRE, LONGING OR NEED HAVE YOU NEVER PUT INTO WORDS?

DO YOU PREFER SPONTANEITY OR PLANNED? WHY?

WHAT ARE YOU TRYING TO STOP DOING, START DOING OR CHANGE? WHY?

HOW CAN YOU CELEBRATE AND REWARD YOURSELF ON A DAILY BASIS? MAKE A LIST, EVERYTHING BIG & SMALL.

Experiment.

WHAT ARE YOU MOST EXCITED ABOUT RIGHT NOW?

WHAT PROMISE WOULD YOU MOST LIKE TO GIVE YOURSELF?

WHAT MAKES YOU FEEL ALIVE?

WHAT DO YOU WANT TO SAY NO TO IN ORDER TO SAY YES TO SOMETHING ELSE?

Embrace

Magick

The Beltane season lasts around six weeks and it's a time to celebrate all the pleasures in being alive. Fill this season with magic, joy, fun, hope and love and make space for lust, passion, sensuality and sexuality.

CELEBRATE LOVE IN ALL ITS FORMS

Beltane is a time for love in all of its forms. The love of friends, family and animals. Romantic, platonic and sensual love, yes all the love. Celebrate love in all its forms — it might be enough to give affection and listen to those you love.

THE FAERIES AND NATURE SPIRITS AWAKEN

Just as at Samhain, which is opposite to Beltane in the Wheel of the Year, the days around the 1st of May is a time when the veil between the worlds is thin. In May you might get a glimpse into the world of faeries and nature spirits.

Pay them your respect by giving them gifts, a flower wreath, crystals or edible seeds.

MAKE A WISH

It is considered very good luck to make wishes on Beltane. Write them down and bury them in fertile soil or write your wishes on colored ribbons and tie them to a tree. Or simply just say your wishes out loud to let the faires hear them.

Litha
POSSIBILITY & CHALLENGE

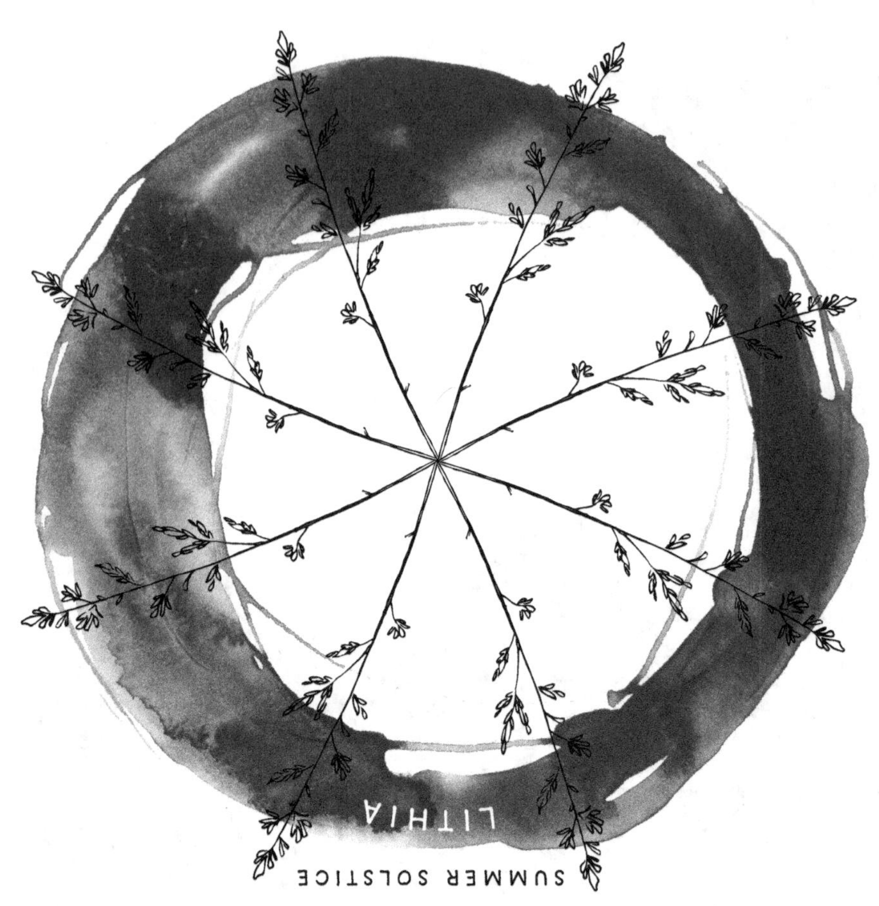

NORTHERN HEMISPHERE

June 20/22 to July 31

SOUTHERN HEMISPHERE

December 20/23 to January 31

Possibility & challenge

Summer Solstice, Litha or Midsummer, a season with many names, all reminding us that the light is at its full strength and potency. A season that can feel challenging or filled with possibility, or both.

It's a time of the year surrounded by a lot of buzz, and expectations. As a swede, I am brought up with very specific ways of doing Midsummer and all the traditions it *should* include.

I would love if this season lets you shine a light on how you feel, be and see this part in the wheel of the year – regardless of the expectations of others. A step, that can in itself, be both a challenge and a possibility.

Enchanted
midsummer

The bright night of Summer solstice comes with mystery and magic. We can imagine fairies dancing in the morning dew, and the forest is filled with life even at night. Be mindful and caring with their presence.

Creating flower wreaths and placing flowers under the pillow to dream of our true love is a tradition familiar to everyone in Sweden, where I live. The root of this tradition has its origin in folklore. The belief was that the plants gathered this night were full of magic and vitality.

Gathering wildflowers is a beautiful way to enjoy the midsummer night. And instead of dreaming about our true love, we can dream about what we want and hope to be able to harvest during the remaining turns of the wheel of the year.

Celebrate the sun and the abundance in nature with a flower mandala. Collect flowers, petals and leaves, and start creating. As you go, release any thoughts of perfection and see if you can enjoy each moment.

As the night is short, light, and hopefully warm, it's a perfect time for rituals outdoors.

At Litha, our focus can be on the powerful energies of the sun. As nature is growing and blooming, it's a great time to expand our own ideas and desires.

Self-compassion

Hmm... did I just make you cringe? Or was the first thought - no, no and another no "ain't gonna do it".

I know, self-compassion can feel like a positivity movement gone over-board. But think again – how does your inner dialogue sound?

When we clear our inner dialogue from judgement, comparison and shame – we allow our own voice to be heard. And, we can begin to navigate from a place of compassion – instead of a constant hustle to convince, compare and compete.

When we tend to ourselves with more compassion and kindness, we tend to everyone and everything around us with a sense of responsibility, curiosity and empathy.

Explore

What does nature look like where you are? What is going on in your surroundings at this time of the year? What are in full bloom? What is still waiting to come alive? How does the wind feel against your skin?

You don't need access to deep forests, unbroken views or even a garden to explore the rhythm of nature. Just step outside and notice how the air feels and affects you.

Paying attention to the changes is another way to begin approaching the rhythm of nature.

If possible, find a tree, some shrubs or a small park that you see more or less on a daily basis and notice the shifts and changes.

Add all senses, the scent of the earth, the colours and how the ground feels beneath your feet.

What signals do you get? How does the energy feel? And does it affect you?

To balance the fiery energy of the sun, we can be in need of adding some water.

If you live near the ocean, a lake, or even a pool – get in! Notice how the water feels when it surrounds your body.

If you rather stay on land, sit by a river or stream and notice the sounds of the water bouncing, swirling and meandering downstream.

And if there are no bodies of water around, hold a glass of water between your hands. Set an intention for what you wish to balance, and let it be transferred into each atom of the water. Drink it – slowly and intentionally.

Observe

Discern

Discover

Nowadays it almost feels natural to focus on what is going on around us and outside us. The updates on social media and news can hold us in a constant state of following, chasing, and looking for outer advice or approval. And other's truths and actions flood our own trust and values.

And frankly – it feels difficult to not look for an answer before checking in with ourselves.

As every garden needs weeding - so do our outer and inner landscape.

Use the energy of this season to create momentum, direction and perspectives, with a foundation coming from how you want to be, feel and operate in your life.

Start with observing the balance of your inner and outer sources of guidance. What appears can feel uncomfortable and maybe even scary - so take your time.

There is no one right way to do this and if you have your own process, stick with it.

If not, the following pages invite you to explore, ponder and discern.

Create your way.

Do it at your pace.

And only if you want to.

WHAT DO YOU HEAR WHEN YOU LISTEN TO THE INITIAL INNER CHATTER?

CAN YOU LET GO BEYOND THE FIRST CHATTER? WHAT DO YOU HEAR?

Observe

HOW WOULD YOU DESCRIBE YOUR INNER DIALOGUE? DOES IT HAVE A TONE, CREATE A FEELING, SOUND LIKE SOMEONE YOU KNOW?

ARE YOU PUSHING SOME THOUGHTS TO THE SIDE-LINE? OVER AND OVER AGAIN? WHY?

IS YOUR INNER VOICE LIFTING YOU UP? HOW? AND IF NOT, WHY?

CAN YOU IDENTIFY THOUGHTS THAT COME FROM YOURSELF, AND THE ONES ORIGI-
NATING FROM SOMEONE ELSE?

Discern

ARE THERE ANY CLASHES BETWEEN WHAT YOU ARE THINKING AND HOW YOU ACT?

WHAT THOUGHTS FEEL BURIED OR FORGOTTEN? IS IT TIME TO BRING THEM INTO THE
LIGHT?

IF NO ONE IS JUDGING, WATCHING OR COMPARING YOU, WHAT DOES YOUR INNER VOICE TELL YOU?

DO YOU SEE YOURSELF DIFFERENTLY WHEN YOU'RE BY YOURSELF? COMPARED TO WHAT YOU THINK ABOUT YOURSELF WHEN YOU ARE AROUND PEOPLE? WHAT DIFFERS?

WHAT THOUGHTS DO YOU NEED TO STOP FORCING OR HAVE MORE PATIENCE WITH?

WHEN DO YOU FEEL GREAT ABOUT YOURSELF? AND CAN YOU NOTICE WHAT CREATES THOSE FEELINGS?

Discover

Magick

As a symbol of the sun and a common shape in nature, the spiral stands in the centre of cyclical living. It can be a symbol of slowly revealing things that are hidden at its core. And it can show us a intentional way of expansion and evolution.

JOURNEY THROUGH THE SPIRAL

The centre of the spiral symbolizes winter solstice, the darkest time of the year. As we spiral outward towards the light, through Imbolc, Ostara and Beltane, the days grow lighter and longer until we reach the very edge - Litha or Summer Solstice. Here the sun stands still before moving us back inward.

Travelling through Lammas, Mabon, Samhain, and the darker days. Returning to the centre, at winter solstice and Midwinter, we pause and rest, before we spiral back outward again.

DEATH AND REBIRTH

The spiralling is also cycles of death and rebirth, change, learning and re-learning. Every cycle comes with new insights, situations, challenges and possibilities.

WALK, MAKE AND CREATE YOUR OWN RITUAL

Right now, at the very edge of the spiral, is a perfect time to reflect on what the journey toward this point has brought. And also what we wish for the journey back inwards.

Create your own spiral of nature materials that are abundant where you live. If you want to walk a spiral, gather material from the ground, cones or stones work perfectly. You can also go on an adventure and look for spirals in your surroundings, they are as common in nature as in architecture.

And if you can't find one - you have one at your fingertips.

Lammas

GATHER THE GOLD

NORTHERN HEMISPHERE

August 1 to September 20/21

SOUTHERN HEMISPHERE

February to March 19/20

Gather the gold

Lammas is the first harvest season of the year. The rolling fields of the landscape are transformed into golden hay bales, and the wildlife that lived protected in the fields become visible again.

In this space between summer and autumn, the energy is still high, but a sense of melancholy might creep in with the slow decrease in light and vitality.

It's the season for harvesting the crops of grain and the seeds from what has bloomed. What has blossomed for you? What is still about to bloom or ripen before it bears fruit?

When harvesting comes the opportunity to gather, sort and sift what we have experienced so far during the year. As well as take note of what we can't harvest, the ideas, projects and thoughts that never happened. From that, we can also "harvest" and gather experience.

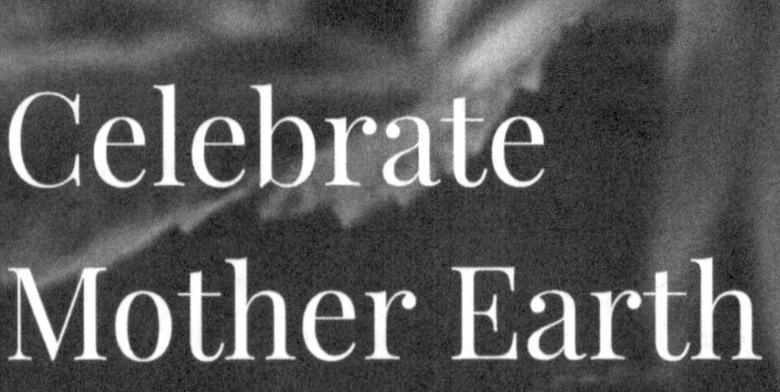
Celebrate
Mother Earth

Lammas, or Lughnasadh, is the cross-quarter point, between midsummer and autumn equinox when Mother Earth is honoured, celebrated and thanked. It is a day to gather friends and loved ones and enjoy the sun's, perhaps final, warmth.

Serve fruit, berries and vegetables, that are in season where you live, as an additional thanks to the earth and the sun.

CELEBRATE MOTHER EARTH

We are all dependent and connected to Mother Earth and what she gives us.

As you enjoy the seasonal harvest, ask yourself how you can care for, re-engage with, and decrease the depletion of our Earths resources.

Explore and decide what small and big habits you can change as a thank you to Mother Earth.

BREAD, HERBS AND SEEDS

The harvest of grain is in focus but, it's also a time to harvest herbs and gather seeds.

Give thanks for the first harvest of the year by baking bread and season it with herbs from your own garden.

Sharing it with others doubles the tribute.

To give up

The difference between letting go, release ourselves from something and give up may seem subtle, but within us, the giving up can feel overwhelming.

Letting go of what no longer serves or works for us often feels liberating. Giving up something we sincerely believed in, wanted or really hoped for, and perhaps made countless attempts to achieve, can feel like a failure.

To identify, with complete transparency and honesty, what it is time to give up, aligns with the essence of this season.

Nature gives up its efforts to sprout and grow in the wrong conditions, the wrong spot or in the wrong soil, and after a while, something new emerges. In nature, there is no failure in giving up; on the contrary, it provides a chance to let something new sprout.

WHAT SEEDS, FROM DREAMS AND IDEAS, DID YOU NEVER SOW? WHY?

ARE THERE A SPECIFIC AREA THAT YOU CAN NOTICE HAS A PATTERN OF NEGLECT? WHY?

Explore

What does nature look like right now where you are? What is going on in your surroundings at this time of the year? What colors does the landscape have? What scent fills the air? And how does the wind feel against your skin?

You don't need to have access to deep forests, unbroken views or even a garden to explore the rhythm of nature. Just step outside and notice how the air feels against your skin, in your nostrils and how it affects you.

Paying attention to the changes in one specific place over time is another way to begin to approach the rhythm of nature.

Add all the senses, the scent of the earth, the colors and how the ground feels beneath your feet.

What signals do you get? How does the energy feel? And does it affect you?

THE CHANGING SEASONS AND SHIFTS IN NATURE AFFECT US ALL BUT IN DIFFERENT WAYS. HOW DO YOU EXPERIENCE THIS TIME BETWEEN SUMMER & AUTUMN? HOW DO YOU REACT AND ACT?

INVIGORATING AND SOOTHING

Collecting and drying herbs to use during autumn and winter is a longtime tradition. The harvest season for a lot of common herbs is right now.

LEMON BALM

Soothing, de-stressing, elevates mood and learning ability and gives sleep a boost.

ROSEMARY

For better memory and concentration, increase blood circulation, soothing in case of anxiety and insomnia.

MINT

Both relaxing and stimulating. The scent increases alertness, memory and gives an energy boost.

SAGE

Stimulates memory and thinking ability, improves mood and relieves blood sugar fluctuations.

Gather
Sort
Sift

Harvesting, literally or figuratively, is more than gather what has grown. To discover the true capacity of our harvest, we also need to sort and sift. The same process the farmer uses, we need to do with our experiences, lessons and perspectives that we have brought with us from the year so far.

When we harvest experiences, we may have a tendency to think they have to be positive and successful. To uncritically take a look at what has transpired without judging or valuing it can be a journey both in our inner and outer lives.

To curiously and openly notice what we did or did not do, who we met, what we did a lot of and what was undone, are all valuable parts of our personal harvest.

I encourage you to during the Lammas' season gather and start sorting and sifting your experiences. And note, what emerges at the first glance may not be the complete picture.

Go deep, dive into the details and do not be seduced by generalizing.

And, let it take time.

WHICH SEEDS WERE PLANTED, NOURISHED AND GREW STRONG? HOW DID YOU AC-COMPLISH THAT? AND WHY DID YOU SUCCEED?

WHEN AND HOW DID YOU MAINTAIN CONFIDENCE IN YOURSELF AND YOUR INTEN-TION?

Gather

WHAT IN YOUR PERSONAL HARVEST SURPRISES YOU? WHY?

**GO BACK TO PAGE 7; CAN YOU NOTICE A CONNECTION BETWEEN WHAT CAME TO LIFE
AND WHAT DID NOT GROW? WHAT ARE THEY?**

Gather

HOW DO YOU NOTICE YOUR OWN TRANSFORMATION?

Sort

WHAT HAS NOT CHANGED? DOES IT FEEL POSITIVE OR NEGATIVE?

WHEN DO YOU FEEL AT EASE WITH EXPLORING NEW WAYS OF BEING? WHY?

WHEN DO YOU FEEL AT EASE WITH NEW WAYS OF THINKING? WHY?

WHEN HAVE YOU FELT LOST OR WITHOUT CONFIDENCE?

WHAT DO YOU WANT TO CONTINUE TO EXPLORE? WHY?

Magick

Rituals help us bring what we have discovered and learned into everyday life. And I know; many people think and believe that rituals are woo-woo, naked dancing around fires or sacrificial offerings to evil spirits. And yes, rituals can be all that, but most of all, they are tools to create focus and presence with a specific purpose.

HABIT, ROUTINE OR RITUAL

Habits and routines are what we do more or less automatically – they create structure and order in our everyday chaos. A ritual, on the other hand, is filled with meaning and purpose through our intention.

What do you want the ritual to help you with? What do you want to achieve by performing a ritual? And who or what can help you?

The simplest of rituals is to light a candle, stop for a moment and say, out loud or in your mind's eye, your intention. Add a symbol or thing that reminds you of the intention throughout the day.

Creating a presence in everyday routines is also a way of doing rituals.

Let the shower water rinse away what you often notice makes you anxious. Let ten minutes of reading be the long-awaited transition from work to free time.

And always in a way that your original intention is reflected and supported.

Mabon

HONOUR DUALITY

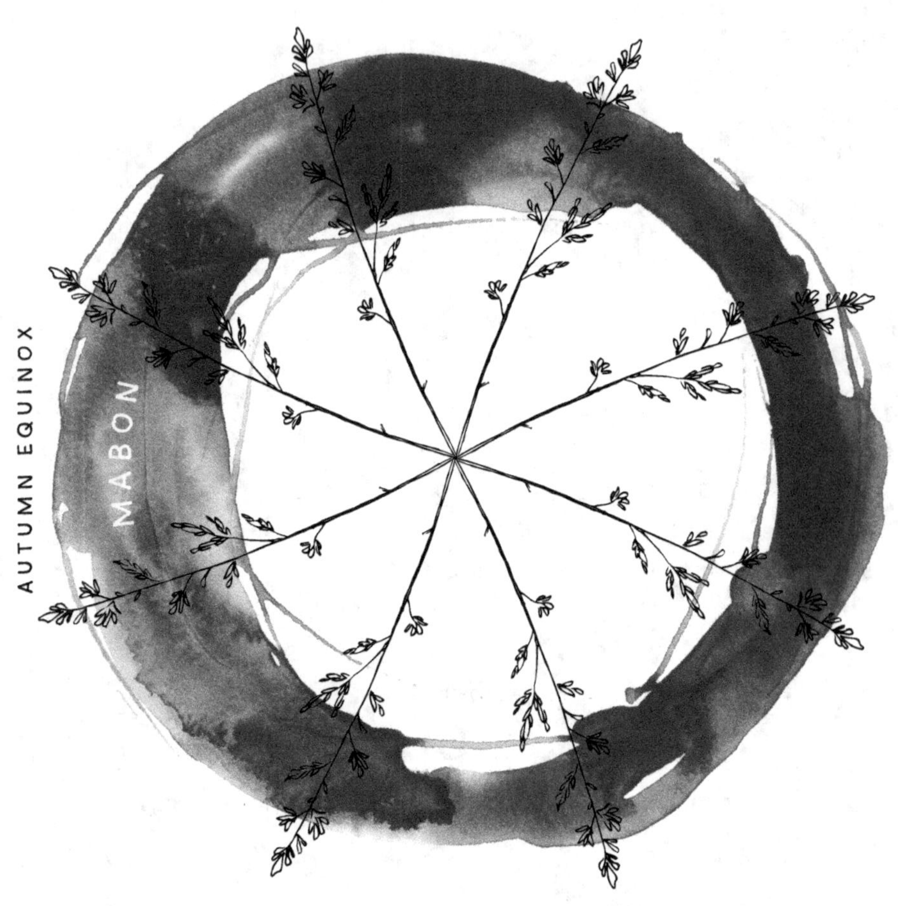

NORTHERN HEMISPHERE

September 22/23 – October 30

SOUTHERN HEMISPHERE

March 20/21 – April 29

Honour duality

At the autumn equinox night and day are, again, of equal length and in equilibrium – dark and light, masculine and feminine, inner and outer, in balance.

We are also on the cusp of transition, from this moment darkness begins to defeat the light. Nature's cycle is moving towards completion. The sap of the trees returns back to their roots, deep into earth, and the green backdrop changes to the fiery colours of autumn.

Before the leaves fall to the ground and decay, we can celebrate what we've accomplished, made happen and achieved, and at the same time, don't be burdened by what didn't happen or wasn't accomplished. We can let go, and at the same time cherish that we did the best we could.

Celebrate
the richness

Mabon marks the official start of Autumn, when day and night are equal in length, and it's also the last season in the Wheel of the Year.

It's a time to pay tribute to Mother Earth for the abundance she brings to this season.

FALL FOR AUTUMN

Get out and into nature – go outside and play in the leaves. Or have a picnic. Get into the forest, or a park, or your (or your neighbours') backyard. Go on a walk and collect autumn trinkets, stop and notice the shift in the air, the temperature and the colours.

CELEBRATE THE RICHNESS

The harvest of fruit and berries are in focus, it's also a time to gather the final crops of vegetables that grow above ground. The branches of the apple trees are weighted down by an abundance of fruit.

Celebrate this day by harvesting something, and use your harvest to cook a meal, bake a pie or make jam or marmalade.

Sharing it adds to the tribute.

Let something die

Autumn can feel demanding, it's a time where Mother Earth clearly signals letting go, decay, death and deep, deep rest. And yet, society at large indicates it's a time to return to work, back to school, a return to doing. It may feel like we are simultaneously being called to rest and called to work.

As humans, we shy away from using the word death, it feels final, the ending of all endings. Turning to nature, we learn that death is a transition and a natural stage in a complete process.

When we reflect on loss, death and the natural cycle of life it's normal to feel sadness and grief. I suggest you allow all the feels.

To let something die opens for what can come next, to grieve and cry is often a much-needed release for body, mind and soul.

WHERE DO YOU FEEL CONSUMED WITH PRESSURES, SHOULDS, COMPARISONS, AND STORIES ABOUT HOW MUCH FURTHER ALONG YOU SHOULD BE THAN YOU ARE.

WHAT ARE YOU READY TO LET DIE?

Explore

What does nature look like right now where you are? What is going on in your surroundings at this time of the year? What colors does the landscape have? What scent fills the air? And how does the wind feel against your skin?

You don't need to have access to deep forests, unbroken views or even a garden to explore the rhythm of nature. Just step outside and notice how the air feels against your skin, in your nostrils and how it affects you.

Paying attention to the changes in one specific place over time is another way to begin to approach the rhythm of nature.

Add all the senses, the scent of the earth, the colors and how the ground feels beneath your feet.

What signals do you get? How does the energy feel? And does it affect you?

BALANCE

I believe we often think about balance as something that can be constant and isn't it the absolute opposite?

Balance is never static; it's shifts, movement, change – it is alive.

To be, feel and have balance in our lives, we need to tend to it in a way that supports us as individuals.

How long is too long, how much is too much? And what do you need to balance what you do too much, too long or rarely.

And take notice if you spend your time constantly chasing balance instead of listening to what you need.

Remember, balance is fluent, always shifting.

How does it feel when you are in balance with your life? Do you discern the opposite?

Cherish
Celebrate
Compost

This last season of the wheel of the year is truly a period of duality: the final sense of warmth, light and summerish energy alongside leaves and temperatures falling, and the entering of darkness.

It's death and life, it's endings and beginnings and an opportunity to reflect on your own journey.

We often discard our accomplishments and move on to the next thing. Give yourself time to celebrate your accomplishments and successes, trials and errors, triumphs and failures.

This is also a perfect season to let things rest, not necessarily abandon them permanently, but to let them fall to the ground, compost and see if they re-emerge.

There is no one right way to do this and if you have your own process, stick with it.

If not, the following pages invite you to explore, ponder and discern.

Create your way.

Do it at your pace.

And only if you want to.

WHAT DID YOU START THAT ENDED UP AS SOMETHING ELSE?

WHAT WOULD YOU LIKE TO CONTINUE WITH? (BEING, DOING, CREATING, FEELING).

WHAT DO YOU FEEL WAS A SUCCESS? NO NEED TO JUST COUNT THE BIG, HUGE
THINGS. TINY STEPS, SMALL WINS AND EVERYDAY HURRAY'S COUNT.

HOW CAN YOU CELEBRATE WHO YOU ARE? (NOT WHO YOU WISH/WANT/THOUGHT
YOU SHOULD/COULD BE – JUST EXACTLY WHO YOU ARE RIGHT NOW).

HOW DO YOU RECOGNIZE, REJOICE AND CELEBRATE YOUR ACCOMPLISHMENTS AND
SUCCESSES?

CAN YOU ADD SMALL CELEBRATIONS TO YOUR EVERYDAY LIFE? HOW WOULD THAT
FEEL? WHY?

ARE YOU CARRYING UNRESOLVED CONFLICTS, OLD GRUDGES OR FEELINGS OF GUILT THAT NEED TO BE DEALT WITH? CAN YOU ADDRESS THEM BEFORE THE FIRST FROST TAKES HOLD OF THEM?

DO YOU HOLD ANY BELIEFS ABOUT NOT BEING OR DOING ENOUGH? WHAT CAN YOU LET GO OF TO BE AND FEEL "ENOUGH"?

Compost

Magick

A jar of blessings can be filled with notes of happy, fun, loving, and memorable moments that happen during the year. It can be small treasures gathered throughout the year that remind you of a place, a day or an experience. These notes, or trinkets, can serve as reminders of joy and wonder in our lives. When we open the jar, we are transported back to those special moments.

Choose a jar (bowl or pot) and create a ritual to charge it with the possibilities of new precious moments. Reflect on what you wish to bring in and how you want to feel, and imagine all of that flowing into your jar.

You can choose to start your jar with small things that represent your wishes or add words and colours that represent them.

A simple spell that is easy to do – but powerful. Gather dry leaves. On each leaf, write something you would like to be rid of.

Crush each leaf in your hand and allow the shreds to be carried off by the wind.

The photos

Dario Brönnimann; page 79

Rachael Gorjestani; page 85

Alex Seinet; page 88

Artur Łuczka; page 91

Sarah Khan; page 100

Gary Bendig; page 101

Pezibear @Pixabay; page 86

Siim Lukka; page 103

Markus Spiske; page 107, 110, 151

Mathias Nevière; page 107

Mila Young; page 108

Aron Burden; page 113

Javier Esteban; page 122

J'Waye Covington; page 123

Bence Balla-Schottner; page 125

Irina Iriser; page 128

Daiga Ellaby; page 129

Niklas Hamann; page 130

Alex Josefsson; 135

Omar Ram; page 144

Lucas Silva Pinheiro Santos; page 145

Tetiana Shyshkina; page 151

Joseph V M; page 152

Phillip L Arking; page 157

Kevin Mueller; page 166

Ksenia Yakovleva; page 167

Omid Armin; page 173

Ellie Ellien; page 173

Irena Carpaccio; page 174

Autumn Mott Rodeheaver; page 178

Zhang K Aiyv; page 188

Heather Ford; page 189

Martin Widenka; page 189

Most photos via Unsplash.com

Thanks!

Typography

PLAYFAIR is designed by Claus Eggers Sørensen, a Danish type designer based in Amsterdam, Netherlands.

It's design lends itself to the late 18th century, and while it is not a revival of any particular design, it takes influence from the designs of John Baskerville and from 'Scotch Roman' designs. [Source: Google Fonts]

NOTO SANS, and the Noto family, is designed with the goal to achieve visual harmony across multiple languages, scripts, and platforms. In all honesty it isn't the ideal choice for print but after some debate I opted to stay with it.

The Latin characters in Noto Sans are based on Droid Sans and Open Sans, fonts designed by Steve Matteson.

The name Noto has a story. "When text is rendered by a computer, sometimes characters display as little boxes because your device doesn't have a font that has images for them, these boxes are known as 'tofu'. The name Noto is to convey Google's goal that users see 'no more tofu'." [Source: Wikipedia]

The author

ANNA LINDER is a Swedish graphic artist, visual poet and book designer. She's also a writer but not quite accepting of that role.

Anna has lived with depression, anxiety, co-dependency, emotional and verbal abuse. She's also experienced healing, the wonders of yoga, the magic in nature and the support of deep feeling conscious women who lead with their hearts.

In 2018, she curated *The Book of Emotions* by calling on women writers and fellow heart leaders, highly sensitives, empaths, and survivors. The book serves as a guide to everybody and anybody who has shut down or lost their internal navigation system in life.

Anna's wish for herself and her readers is to navigate life with more ease through identifying the innate feelings and rhythms of our body, mind, and soul.